Introduction

This is a book of 31 meditations. You can read one meditation a day for a month or read a meditation whenever you may need insight into a particular topic. The theme of the meditations is self-discovery. Truth is powerful and takes awhile to penetrate self-doubt, our unique confusions, and our negative self-talk. The meditations are often more personal and powerful after repeated readings. Reflect on the truth each meditation holds for you right now. A month from now you may be ready to accept another truth so re-reading might be beneficial. Some truths are repeated in different meditations because they are critical for our growth. The meditations are offered in a most humble spirit. We are traveling this journey together. I hope these meditations encourage you.

Refuse To Be Defined By Your Past

Make a pact with yourself today not to be defined by your past. We grew up in a world of confusion. Adults seemed scary. Uncles, aunts, and neighbors appeared to be in on a secret that we were not. Teachers were often intimidating. School administrators were threatening. Who could we turn to for help? We had meager resources. Our peers were just as confused and clueless. Is it any wonder we messed up? We were traveling through strange territories with no map, no guide and lots of false intelligence. We had to make colossal decisions in the spur of the moment: who to let touch our bodies, what substances to put in our bodies, who we could trust, who we couldn't trust, what houses were safe to enter, who was telling us the truth, which of our friends was capable of betraying us, and dozens more. Our own likes and dislikes were being developed on the run. Is it any wonder we made mistakes? We had to make many of these decisions with people we were just randomly growing up with- people we may not have known a year later. We had no one to ask for honest advice. And the more dysfunctional our family of origin, the younger we found ourselves in these confusing situations. Forgive yourself right now for anything you did before you gained the wisdom to know any better. It wasn't your fault.

If You're Not Changing Your Mind Frequently...

If you're not changing your mind frequently, maybe you're not using it right. Too many decisions are made unconsciously. We are at the mercy of powerful impulses we spend a lifetime trying to understand. Have you ever awakened on Sunday morning wincing immediately at your memories of Saturday night? We have every intention of staying on the path, practicing peace, making smart decisions, following good orderly direction and yet... there are those mornings we anxiously hope what we are remembering is only a dream. But things that hurt, instruct. Point yourself in a better direction with renewed vigor and hard-earned wisdom.

We can also change our opinions any time we feel moved to do so. We can change teams, candidates, hairstyles, fashion, and choice of friends. No one has to agree with our choices. We have to live with them. Trust yourself. You can always change your decision again if it doesn't feel right. Trees that are flexible when heavy winds blow usually survive the storm. Trees that appear more stable and substantial are often uprooted during fierce storms because they are inflexible. Flexibility of both mind and body is essential if we are to survive the storms of life.

Don't ever feel like you've painted yourself into a corner. Family and friends may try to insist that you remain stagnant because it is easier for them to deal with a one-dimensional person. That is their issue, not yours. We witness changes in the natural world every season and we are part of that world. Stay fluid and dynamic.

Forgiveness Frees Us

Forgiveness is a difficult task. Why should someone who has hurt us so much be forgiven? Who can blame us for being resentful for the hurt that was inflicted upon us? How about the times when we forgave someone only to be hurt again and again? The answer to these questions always boils down to this: are we really "getting even" with anyone by continuing to hold hostile feelings towards them? Hostile feelings hurt us at the cellular level. Hostile feelings make us ill. Haven't we been hurt enough already? Why should this person steal our health and happiness even now? What if there was a way to make certain that this person never hurts us again?

Try this: forgive, forget and move on. This is the only way to guarantee that the damage done by this person is in the past. We are clear of this person in the present. We are clear of this person in the future. All we need to do is summon up the courage and determination to take this challenging step: forgiving and forgetting. Then we'll let go of anger and resentment and other emotions that harm our health. We are free of any lingering connection to negative, hurtful people. We become lighter and healthier simply by letting go. Sever your connection once and for all by forgiving and moving forward.

Isn't it great that this person will never again be part of your life? Free yourself right now.

Keep Our Eyes On The Prize

What practical steps can we take to improve our life? The first step is quieting our minds and realizing that thoughts are not true. Thoughts are random events. Many are true and many are echoes of negative voices from our past. Choose thoughts that empower you. Let the negative thoughts dissolve. They aren't true.

When are minds are peaceful, we can reflect on where we want to go in life. What is our purpose? What dreams about our future energize and excite us? Where would we like this journey to lead? With that intention firmly in our mind, we take the first logical step to moving toward our goal. Then we take the next step. We keep our eyes on the prize and continue in a good, orderly direction towards a rewarding and soul-nourishing future, our future. We may have to move on from former friends or we may be fortunate enough to have fiends who will support and encourage our new dream. Decide which friends are coming and keep moving forward. Shed all negative influences that could hold you back.

Once you are focused on a goal, doors will open and powerful forces will assist you. Some day when you are much older you will look back and your life's journey will seem as perfectly constructed as a great novel. Make improvements to your diet and commit to daily physical and spiritual exercises that will keep you clean and clear. Keep your eyes on the prize. Do something every day that moves your life toward a happier, more rewarding future..

Accept Life On Life's Terms

What does it mean to accept life on life's terms? It means we are committed to reality and truth. We fully accept our present circumstances as they are. We no longer complain because our circumstances are not what they "should be." If we are not completely dedicated to reality, we are wasting time and energy that could be devoted to change. We accept the people around us exactly as they are and realize in the core of our being that we are not here to change anyone else but us. What we see is what we get. Accept a person they way they are or walk away and wish them well in their personal struggle to change. Acknowledge that we are completely powerless to change another person. Trying to change someone else is a substitute for the legitimate struggle to change ourselves. The impulse to change someone else is a diversion from the very challenging task of changing ourselves.

We cannot change the past. If we must make amends or apologize for past deeds, we make them and return immediately to spending our energy moving our life in a more positive direction. If the person we made a sincere apology to demands further apology, that's their issue. Move forward and stay dedicated to resolving your own issues. What positive, realistic steps can you take today to move your life closer to your goals and dreams?

Worry Has Yet to Solve
A Single Problem

Worry has yet to solve a single problem. It saps our energy and makes it less likely that we will be successful confronting any challenge. Worry makes us weaker, not stronger. It has a negative impact on our health. Worrying that we will not be up to a task is self-defeating. We have resources that we never realized and we can grow these resources by facing this challenge.

Trust yourself and trust that invisible powers support you. Worrying displays a lack of trust in our strengths and talents. Stay strong. You are stronger than ever. You are wiser than ever. Past defeats have been great teachers and now you are armed with new insights. You have never been better prepared to face a challenge. Stop any negative thought before it takes root. Breathe deeply and assure yourself that you already possess every necessary trait and talent to surmount any obstacle. We always manage better with a calm mind. Focus on maintaining a calm, peaceful mind and banish all negativity.

Appreciate that you are here to believe and achieve. Your life is your mission. Visualize your goal and see yourself achieving your goal. Take the first steps today and know that you will be provided with the energy, the insight, the courage and the power to succeed. No one can do your part except you and you have been given all of the tools and talents to succeed. Believing is seeing.

No Longer Be Held Back By Fear

Our spirits are living forces that we can sense if we quiet our minds and become peaceful. Our spirits will inspire us and guide us. When we accept their guidance, we are provided with energy sufficient to meet any challenge that confronts us. We are continually encouraged to grow and expand. If we refuse, our psyche protests and we experience physical symptoms such as headaches, upset stomachs, and blurred vision. We could experience emotional symptoms such as depression. We have disturbing dreams. But the only way out is through. Our spirit understands that we are frequently the chief obstacle that we are challenged to overcome. Please do not let your life be governed by fear. Our fears are our true enemies. Other people do not stand between us and success- we do. Our fears may convince us we are not up to the task but we are built for the challenge.

Our so-called enemies are governed by fear too. If we understand that, it is easier to forgive them and loosen their hold on us. Then we realize that the only thing standing in our way is not other people but rather our own doubts about our strengths and abilities. Fear is our real enemy. Fear shrinks our world. Do you want to grow larger or smaller? Trust yourself and promise yourself that you life will no longer be held back by fear.

Take The Next Step Forward

Take the next step forward. Refuse to let the past hold you back. Today is a new day and a new life filled with new possibilities. It's a moment of keen insight when we realize that burdens from the past have been weighing us down in the present. But don't play the blame game. Blaming people for their own unconscious actions is a waste of time because it doesn't move your own life forward. Keep moving forward. Keep your eyes on the prize. Where are you going in life? You can't move forward by looking backwards. Promise yourself that you will no longer use your past history for your lack of action today. Get moving. You are no longer trapped. You are free to be who you want to be. Hold a positive image in your mind. Don't let anyone taint you. Don't let anyone deter you. So many people are stuck because they don't have the imagination necessary to achieve success. Find the path that leads to where you want to be. Be courageous. Ask someone who has been there how she got there. We all have to find the courage to travel the path ourselves but it never hurts to ask someone for directions. Now that you've shed resentment and blaming, you will travel much lighter. The longest journey begins with a single step. Take that step today. You are on your way to achieving your dreams.

Develop Clear Boundaries

Don't take other people's bad habits, bad manners, or rudeness personally. Their actions are about that person, not you. Stay clear of other people's issues and confusion. It's difficult enough trying to deal with our own. Develop clear boundaries. Don't become tainted by other people's issues. And don't let your ego look for reasons to feel offended.

People love stories. We spend our hard-earned dollars on books and movies because we enjoy the narrative elements. But don't let your mind develop a similar narrative and backstory every time you feel offended. Most offenses begin and end with the simple fact that we ran into someone in a bad mood and they insulted us somehow. The story is about them and their bad mood and has nothing to do with us. Our egos love encouraging us to feel offended. Maybe it makes us feel important. If no one has been rude to us in the current day, our ego will scan the past for real or imagined slights. How about this? How about that? Don't you remember when this person made plans without you? Why are you being nice to them when they offended you last month? We can never be sure of another person's motivations, can we? It's challenging enough trying to decipher our own. Let other people deal with their issues while we focus on finding peace.

Whose Story Are You Living?

Whose story are you living? Does it originate from your own center or are you still being pulled into the gravity of someone else's story, someone else's fantasy? When we are young, it's difficult not to conform to other people's expectations, whether realistic or not. We must adhere to our parent's wishes or face the consequences. We are dependent on our parents for so much that we may not realize we are not dependent on them to suggest a career or lifestyle. Their advice may be well intended but is still a part of their dream.

It would be perfectly natural for a parent to say, "I always dreamed you'd become a doctor," or express some other unconscious fantasy of theirs. But our lives pass quickly and we aren't here to fulfill anyone's dreams but our own. If you find yourself in the wrong story, leave. Develop your own dreams, your own personal narrative. Where are you headed? No one will get you there except you. Choose a point on some future horizon and take the steps necessary to get there. It's no secret how any career goal is achieved. Read a book, ask a career or guidance counselor, do research online. Take responsibility for your own future. Live your own dreams. Be willing to do the work to make your dreams come true. If you are just awakening from living a life that other people planned for you, spend time alone and get to know yourself better. What do you truly want from this wonderful, too brief life?

Whose Issues Are These?

Young kids often claim other children's toys in nursery schools and swim clubs. Adults are sometimes just as stubborn about claiming things that are not rightfully theirs. We are responsible for dealing with our own issues, feelings and failings. And it is essential that we let our loved ones own their issues. If someone we love has an addiction or another self-defeating behavior, we have to detach with love. It's their issue, not ours. If a family member is manipulative or constantly angry or drowning in some other negativity, detach. It has nothing to do with you. We are responsible for accepting the consequences of our actions. Other people, even people whom we love greatly, are responsible for accepting the consequences of their actions. It's not our behavior and it's far beyond our powers to try to buffer or soften the consequences of someone else's negative behavior.

Other people's abusive behaviors, deceptions, manipulations, and dishonesties belong to them, not us. Detach with love and move in a positive direction. Let other people deal with the issues they have created. We are responsible for any problem that we caused. They are responsible for any problem that they caused. Escape from the web of any loved one's deceitful, manipulative, addictive or self-destructive behavior. You don't belong there. It's sad and upsetting to witness; but it has nothing to do with you. Stay peaceful and accept that you are responsible for only you. Detach with love and move forward.

Thoughts Aren't Real

Thoughts aren't real. Thoughts aren't true. Some thoughts have a valid meaning to us and we can give our attention to these thoughts and weigh exactly how meaningful they are for us. Other thoughts are not true and have no meaning at all for us. They can be ignored because they provide no benefit to our lives. In fact, they are intrusive. Nuisance thoughts can be disturbing and are best ignored. We can tell our minds to "stop" the flow of any thoughts that seem bothersome. It is essential to develop a firm sense of who we are so that we can stop the flow of thoughts that are not congruent with our identity. We are often hounded by thoughts that try to tell us we are unworthy. These thoughts are untrue; ignore them. We are occasionally plagued by thoughts that try to tell us we are imposters and just pretending to be competent. These thoughts are untrue; ignore them. We are bothered by thoughts that try to tell us we don't deserve the good that we have already earned. These thoughts are untrue; ignore them .We are worthy. We have earned our successes. We have achieved a high degree of competence or we would have stumbled long ago. We deserve the good that we've been blessed with because we have blessed others through our good deeds. Shakespeare said our thoughts are traitors. Be true to yourself and do not tolerate traitors undermining your sense of who you are.

Living Our Soul's Purpose

It is not surprising that we label certain transcendent musical or dramatic performances as being "soulful." Our souls enter this earthly plane with us at birth and animate our journey along the way. The word "animate" derives from the Latin word "anima" which means "to en-soul." When we live a life congruent with our soul's purpose, we feel invigorated and harmonious. We feel supportive energy that propels us to a purposeful life. We realize that our lives are meaningful. When we find it difficult to connect to our soul's energy, we experience emotional pain and frequently seek ways to distract us from our pain, which can lead to compulsions and addictions. It is essential to calm and quiet our minds and attempt to discern our soul's purpose. It's essential to ask ourselves what will truly give us genuine happiness. Often we are prompted to pursue a path that may "disappoint" our family and friends. No matter. What good is it if we gain the entire world but lose our soul in the process? We will be provided with an abundance of energy to follow our unique path through life as long as we sense we are living our soul's purpose. Living soulfully means that we share our unique gifts with the world each day. We may or may not be rewarded with earthly riches but we will be rewarded with a deep sense of satisfaction and a sincere feeling that our lives are purposeful. Quiet your mind. Look within and discover where your soul's energy is pulling you.

We Are Responsible For Our Own Happiness

Our partners and loved ones are not responsible for our happiness. They are responsible for their own happiness and we are responsible for our own happiness. If we feel unhappy, our loved one is not to blame. Blaming is a waste of time that should be spent seeking peace. The truth is simple: we feel satisfied and happy when our thoughts are peaceful. We feel dissatisfied and unhappy when are thoughts are not peaceful. When our thoughts become agitated and begin to fluctuate between anger and revenge, we should immediately focus on restoring our minds to peace. Strategies such as "getting even" are futile and will only lead to lingering unhappiness. Do we really have the intention to become calm and peaceful? Have we grown addicted to the rush we feel when we are enraged? Do we realize we are making choices that will shorten our life? Do we remember that all moods pass? Do we remember how much grief our anger has caused us in the past? Are we willing to negatively complicate our lives, sometimes for a time much longer than our bad mood is likely to last? Has our anger and refusal to seek peace sometimes turned the tables so that we are the person who ends up making amends and asking forgiveness? Make an intention to find a way to calm yourself whenever you lose your peace.

We Can't Control Other People

Worrying about the choices that other people make is futile. We can't control other people. It's challenging enough trying to control our impulses. How could we possibly control anyone else's? Have you ever made a firm resolution to diet, only to see your strong intentions derailed by a holiday dinner? Have you ever made up your mind to stop cursing because it doesn't project the image you want? That good intention is often forgotten the next time we unconsciously respond to frustration. If it is difficult to change ourselves, we must acknowledge the impossibility of changing someone else. Trying to change anyone else will inevitably frustrate us. If we are confused about why we keep breaking our own resolutions, imagine how confusing it will be trying to prod another person to follow resolutions we have devised for them. It hardly matters that you are suggesting a healthier, more positive lifestyle for a family member or friend. It's their health and it's their life. Our influence stops far short of changing them. Our frustration with this impossible task may lead to worry and anger on our part, damaging our health and subtracting from our energy. We can find ourselves in a worry rut if we spend time obsessing about another's choices. Even if their choices impact us, let's acknowledge that we deserve to be free of harmful practices. Worrying harms us. Poor choices may harm a loved one but hard experiences are often required to wake someone up—not our fretting and nagging.

Stretch Your Mind and You Expand Your World

Stretching your mind will invigorate your life. We graduate from high school having been force fed a diet of ideas, books, philosophies and theories that our parents and teachers found useful to help order their own lives. However, it is up to us to develop ideas that are useful to help order our own lives. It is unlikely, given the difference in age and generational outlook, that our parents' or teachers' philosophies will be all we ever need to navigate our one-of-a-kind life. After we leave high school, we must find our unique path. We leave the collectives of our families and schools and embark on a personal journey. Stretching our mind becomes imperative. Go to a bookstore or public library and explore sections that you may not even have been aware of until now. See if anything captures your interest. If you attend college, use one of your electives to take a course in world religions or Beat period literature or yoga. Stretch your mind. Go see a foreign movie at the local art theatre. Watch something quirky on your local cable movie library. Expand your mind. Check out a different genre of music on your streaming service. Attend church with a friend. You are not betraying anyone or making any commitment. You are exploring. If you stretch your mind, you will stretch your world.

Inspired Is In-Spirit

Inspired means you are in-spirit. When we align ourselves with our soul's purpose, we become energized. We discover talents that have been dormant. We can access powerful forces to assist us on our journey. Observe the powerful surges and subtle miracles of nature. The same powers that make the seas surge flow through us.

We witness this power in peak performance athletes or talented musicians. We have access to the same flow of power. Make your mind receptive to new possibilities and to consciously call these powers into play in your life. Maximize your potential by aligning yourself with the power of the universe: seek wisdom, exercise, live life on life's terms, and seek direction within. If this power can change an acorn into a massive tree and an apple blossom into an apple, it can provide all of the strength you need to achieve your dreams.

Quiet your mind and get in touch with your spirit—you will feel inspired. Gather your creative energies and focus on your goals. Life can be a lonely struggle when we are convinced by our ego that we don't need help from any other source. Quiet your mind. Try to sense the stirrings of your spirit. What are you here for? Certainly not to live the selfish, self-centered life directed by our ego. Leave that lonely life behind. You will be energized by invisible powers as surely as the wind. Stay in harmony with your spirit. We witness miracles every day in the natural world and we are an integral part of the natural world. Your miracle begins now.

Stretch Your Body and Prolong Your Life

Stretching your body will prolong your life. Our bodies need to be stretched. Stretching has been an integral part of athletic warm-ups for so long that it is curious that we don't bring that discipline into our daily lives. We are as young as our spines are flexible. Think of people who have reached their seventh or eighth decade. Those who are still youthful and vigorous are flexible and pliant. Older people who have lost their youthfulness are stiff and rigid. Develop a practice of stretching that will keep you vigorous throughout all of your years. Yoga is the practice of quieting our minds while stretching our bodies. It will bring amazing, positive changes to your life. You will feel more graceful and at ease with your body off the mat because of the hours you have devoted to your practice on the mat. Cats stretch. Dogs stretch. Animals move with a relaxed ease. Do you? We are as young as our spines are flexible. Yoga classes are held in colleges, high schools, YMCA's, gyms, churches, and in thousands of dedicated yoga studios. Classes for beginners are held daily. Find a gentle, encouraging teacher who moves at a pace that makes you feel comfortable. Thousands of yoga videos are available online. Use these videos if you feel self-conscious about practicing in public. Hundreds of great yoga books are available to assist you. Practice at your own pace, but practice. We are as young as our spines are flexible.

Choose Your Mood

Is there a healthy way to alter our mood? Sometimes we sense that darkness has descended upon us. The world suddenly looks gloomy for no identifiable reason. Is there anything we can do to redirect ourselves to a more positive focus? The first thing we can do is to acknowledge that no one else is responsible for our mood but us. A positive first step is to absolve all other people from blame for the darkness we are experiencing, particularly our loved ones. We are in a dark mood because of the inner workings of our unconscious mind, not because our children's grades are less than ideal or our spouse forgot to put the laundry in the dryer. Our answer always is found within. Pointing our finger at others only extends the time we spend in this uncomfortable mood. The first step forward is to begin counting our blessings. Who loves us? Who depends on us? Whom do we love? Which of our friends always comes through for us? Do we appreciate music? Art? Literature? Sports? Great meals? Fitness activities? How much joy do our children bring us? Our grandkids? We have so much to be grateful for.

Breathe deeply and be thankful that we have so many ways to nourish our souls and bodies. Practice gratitude. Don't cling to the darkness. Breathe deeply and walk in the light. Stay strong and coax yourself out of the gloom. An attitude of gratitude will leads to light, love and laughter. You are in charge.

Rehashing and Rehearsing (self-poisoning)

The cells in your body react to everything your mind thinks. Every time we think a negative thought it's as if we swallowed a poison. Next time you are angry or frustrated, step back a moment, catch your breath, and feel the weakness spread throughout your immune system. It's poison. You chose to feel worse at this moment than you did the moment before. Choose peace over revenge. You'll live longer. Let go of old grudges. Carrying a grudge may be dangerous to your health. Anger is a valid human emotion and sometimes it serves us to experience anger in order to realize that someone is taking advantage of us or that we have been unjustly wronged. If this wrong is occurring in the present moment, feel the emotion and draw a boundary.. But if you are rehashing and rehearsing in your mind what you should have said yesterday or last week or last year, let go of the grudge, return to health and choose to remain peaceful. You'll live longer. You'll love longer. You'll laugh longer. You'll feel better. You'll feel lighter. You will no longer be swallowing poison in the hope that the perceived enemy will feel worse. He won't. You will. Let go of the heavy burdens that you are carrying and walk in peace and in light. Smile.

Our Lives Change When Our Thoughts Change

Our lives change when our thoughts change. It's as simple as that. We are never going to receive what we don't feel we deserve. We will push love away to keep our hearts protected and love offerings will be repelled. Love and caring friendships will not be ours until we can envision ourselves being worthy of them. Thousands of thoughts float into our consciousness every day. Some of them are true and some of them are crazy, aren't they? Which thoughts do you give attention to? Which ones do you believe? Promise yourself to focus on your thoughts that support you and encourage you to continue moving in a positive direction. Ignore the untrue thoughts that make you feel undeserving. Ignore all thoughts that may have originated from small-minded, hurting people who pushed their own negative feelings on your innocent mind. This criticism came from adults who were still suffering from the negative impact of their own childhood. If you had a hurting person as a parent, they may have lashed out at you because they did not understand how to process their own pain. Hurt people hurt people. Begin healing yourself right now by attending to thoughts that encourage you to face new challenges. Focus on thoughts that say you are worthy of success, deserving of love always, and open to all of life's many blessings. Change your thoughts and your life will change, your dreams will change, and your future will change. Try it.

Believe in Yourself

If we decide that life is too challenging or too scary, we can rest for a while. If we rest too long, however, our spirits may begin to feel depressed. Our spirits want to soar and to grow. They will allow us, even encourage us, to pause sometimes and regain our strength and renew our commitment to growth. But they will not allow us to give up. We may begin to feel pressed down, depressed. We are programmed to grow and evolve. That is easy to see in the physical world but it's just as true in the spiritual world. Our spirits evolve right along with our bodies and if we refuse to grow spiritually because we are scared or intimidated, our spirits feel pressed down.

Life is very challenging at times. Growth often invokes anxiety. We wonder if we will be up to the task. Are we strong enough to meet this challenge? Do we have enough inner strength? Are we tough enough? Smart enough? Disciplined enough? The only way to find out is to take on the challenge. Our spirit always will support us. The anxiety of growing is always preferable to the depression caused by a refusal to evolve or progress. Have faith in yourself. Realize that your life has brought you to this crossroad because your spirit knows you possess the strength, the intelligence, and the courage to master this new challenge. Believe in yourself and get moving.

Why Do We Accept Less Than We Deserve?

Why do we accept less than we deserve? Were we that desperate for love and affection? Did we allow our physical attraction to someone to blind us to the fact that we were not emotionally suitable for each other? Did we witness neglect or abuse in our parents' relationship and unconsciously assume that is the norm? Did we feel we weren't worthy of someone's full love and support? Did we believe we were capable of "fixing" another person?

We deserve unconditional love and support. We deserve to be appreciated just as we are. We aren't responsible for any other person's behavior; they are. We can't provoke someone who truly loves us to become abusive. They own that behavior, not us. We will never again feel desperate for another's love and affection if we learn to love ourselves.

What steps can we take so that we never accept less than we deserve again? The first step is learning to feel comfortable when we are alone. Get to know yourself before you attempt to get to know anyone else. Know what you are looking for before you go looking. Learn to study another person before becoming emotionally attached. Ask mutual friends to honestly tell you how they feel about someone you begin to admire. Get to know the person as a friend before your relationship becomes serious. Don't be in any great hurry because you are perfectly complete by yourself. Promise yourself you will never again accept less than you deserve.

It's Our Thoughts That Disrupt Our Peace

The only way to find lasting peace is to quiet our mind. Our thoughts disrupt our peace. Lasting happiness begins with a peaceful mind. Buying a new car may bring a strong burst of happiness. We can enjoy it greatly but realize that it will be short lived. New acquisitions may bring a smile to our face but we must acknowledge from past experiences that they will not bring us a peace of mind that will last. Even if they could, it is impossible to spend our lives acquiring new things. If money could buy happiness, wealthy people would be happier than you and me and they are not. Material objects cannot produce a calm mind.

Affairs of the heart will often make us ecstatic but won't produce lasting peace. Many of us are fortunate and blessed by caring, loving partners but still must find lasting peace within. New jobs, great vacations, the successes of our children and loved ones, newborn babies, our favorite sports team winning a championship, job promotions and winning lottery tickets all produce bursts of happy feelings. But even these peak moments dissipate and we are back to the ebb and flow of life. A calm, clear mind brings peace and happiness. A calm, clear mind can be achieved through yoga, meditation and other reflective arts that encourage us to look inwardly for peace by learning to calm our thoughts. A calm, peaceful mind leads to a calm, peaceful life.

Give Yourself Permission To Be Who You Are

Give yourself permission to be who you are. You do not need anyone else's permission. Just yours. Your family doesn't have to like it. They will come around to accept it if you're patient. It's unfortunate that you may have to be patient with them but it takes longer for some people's minds to expand than others. They may be living a script drilled into them by their family of origin and it may take a little while for them to grow enough to accept the whole of you. The good news is that after people widen their viewpoint, it becomes impossible to go back to a narrower way of thinking.

It is the task of our friends and family members to figure out who they are—not who you are. Our souls have a profound desire to grow to our full potential. Don't let anyone hold you back. Don't let grudges from the past to narrow your own thinking in the present. What are you thinking about grudges for? You have a big task right in front of you that requires all of your energy and attention—to become you. We are responsible for our own lives. Please don't be frightened or intimidated. Choose the path that allows you to reach your full potential. Do not allow other people's narrow-minded judgments to constrict you or restrict you. Be strong enough and mature enough to realize that you have a unique gift to bring to the world. Choose the path that enlarges you.

Intimacy

If we are in an intimate relationship where we can truly be our broken self, still loved despite all of our contradictory impulses, fractured parts, fears and phobias, we are deeply blessed. Relationships usually begin tenuously and warily with both parties protecting themselves from feeling vulnerable and exposed. The concept of personality comes from the Greek word for mask, persona. We might wear one mask at work, another with our families of origins, another with our friends. We feel the need to wear masks to hide our inner selves. When we were young and completely vulnerable, we would be our true selves happily and innocently; this led to criticism and censure form our teachers, angry attacks from our parents, and teasing from our peers. Is it any wonder that we quickly learned to construct a series of masks to camouflage our true selves and protect our souls from hurt and pain? By the time we are mature enough for a relationship, we have been hurt, wounded, damaged, misunderstood, rejected and criticized many, many times. Even when we meet someone whom we are physically and emotionally attracted to, our memories of all of the pain inflicted upon us makes us wary and defensive. When we first draw close to someone, we are both on guard. We learn to gradually drop our masks and expose our vulnerable inner selves slowly and slowly and slowly. Intimacy is a courageous act in the face of a lifetime of past hurts and disappointments.

Broken (Part 1)

The Rolling Stones sang about a woman headed for her 19th nervous break-down. That may have been an exercise in cruel hyperbole, but I have known a number of good people who suffered an emotional collapse. "Nervous break-down" is more a figurative term than literal. Each of us has an imaginative map that we trust conforms to the world we know. We have devised our map based on previous experiences, future expectations, assumptions of what our family, friends, neighbors and coworkers expect from us, and our own expectations of the emotional and financial rewards the world will pay us for our efforts. Our map also contains an expectation of returned affection from those people we have given so much of our own affection. We have been taught that we can ex-pect an equal return for all of our physical and emotional efforts. We will get what we give. But if we experience a profound betrayal –if we lose a job where we have invested decades of toil, or if an intensely loved partner is unfaithful, or a loved one passes away—we often feel unmoored. What we are experiencing does not match up with long held beliefs about fairness, loyalty, and reciprocal trust. Our worldview is shattered. We may feel abandoned by God, a loved one, or our employer and we are become so devastated we suffer an emotional implo-sion. Our trusted worldview has "broken down." How do we respond?

Broken (Part 2)

It seems counterintuitive but an emotional breakdown often leads us to a wider, more expansive view of life. As we revise our maps, we gain wisdom. We hope that we've gained more accurate insights and shed some of our naïve notions. Please know that you can rise from any failure. You will be a larger, stronger person. Stay peaceful and regain your equilibrium. What roles that make you feel stifled can be discarded? What roles and behaviors now seem inauthentic? Have you gained a better understanding of who you truly are? What were behaviors you performed just to gain love, appreciation, or employment? Are you ready to step into a bigger, more authentic role in life? Do you feel ready to command more respect and no longer plead for people's affection? Are you tired of begging for someone's love? You are strong. Stay strong. Make a promise to yourself not to be defined by your past. Be who you really are. Realize that not everyone is going to like you and appreciate you but that's not important. You have learned to love yourself more strongly and unconditionally and are less dependent on the approval of others. Maybe you want to take your life in a completely different direction. You are being truly reborn. You may come to understand your emotional implosion as the collapse of false identity scaffolding that your spirit could no longer support. Your breakdown may serve the greater purposes of your spirit and lead you to a happier future.

There Is Always A Way Out

When the way out of a dilemma involves facing thorny legal issues, we may feel intimidated and paralyzed. But there is always a way out. It may not be easy. It may not happen as quickly as we prefer. At times, it may feel so imposing that success seems impossible. We might not have any allies in this struggle. But there is always a way out. The first step in overcoming any daunting task is to prioritize our goals. What should we tackle first? This point is critical for our success. What is the very step to recover our emotional, financial or physical balance? If we quiet our mind, use our innate wisdom, and have a firm intention to succeed, an intelligent, logical first step will become clear. Our first step may be to research where we can obtain free legal advice so that we get a grasp on the legal realities of our predicament. That is a sometimes the most valid and intelligent move we can make: to separate fact from fear and fantasy. Once we have obtained the facts, we can ask advice from people who have experience with our problem. We then can formulate our next step based on our intuition and the wisdom we have gathered. Settling legal matters, making amends, and demonstrating good faith continue our momentum. Be true to your word. The only way out is through. Please don't lose faith in yourself. Trust that you possess all qualities necessary to succeed. You are going to put these problems behind you.

Inner Peace

We spend so much time working to improve our outer appearance and often neglect our inner life. We want to look our best. Do we really want to feel our best? We spend money on clothing, footwear, and jewelry. We hope that a great haircut just might be the change that turns our life in a more positive and fulfilling direction. We debate what brand of jeans flatters us. We may give more attention to our nails than to our inner life. We spend precious time gazing at outerwear ads and trying to imagine how they would improve our appearance. We spare no expense when it comes to skin care and makeup. We litter our bedroom floors with impulsively rejected outfits that fell short of presenting the perfect image we hope to present to the world. We fret about the slightest blemish on our skin. Any and all adjustments to our physical appearance are anguished over as if they genuinely could make life happier or more fulfilling. What about our inner life? Do we have a regimen each day to calm our minds and thoughts? Many people feel that inner beauty is often reflected in our eyes. Are your eyes shining from within? Thirty minutes a day of meditation and yoga will bring more happiness than beauty regimens, wardrobes, expensive jewelry, watches, jeans or haircuts. Give yourself a month to learn about a regimen that may finally give you the peace and security you seek. You deserve peace.

49245165R00020

Made in the USA
Middletown, DE
11 October 2017